I Love Animals

Crazy Colouring For Kids **Book 3**

First published in 2015 by Kyle Craig Publishing

Copyright © 2015 Kyle Craig Publishing

Design: Elizabeth James, Julie Anson, Alison McNicol, Shutterstock, Inc.

ISBN: 978-1-78595-097-1

A CIP record for this book is available from the British Library.

A Kyle Craig Publication

www.kyle-craig.com

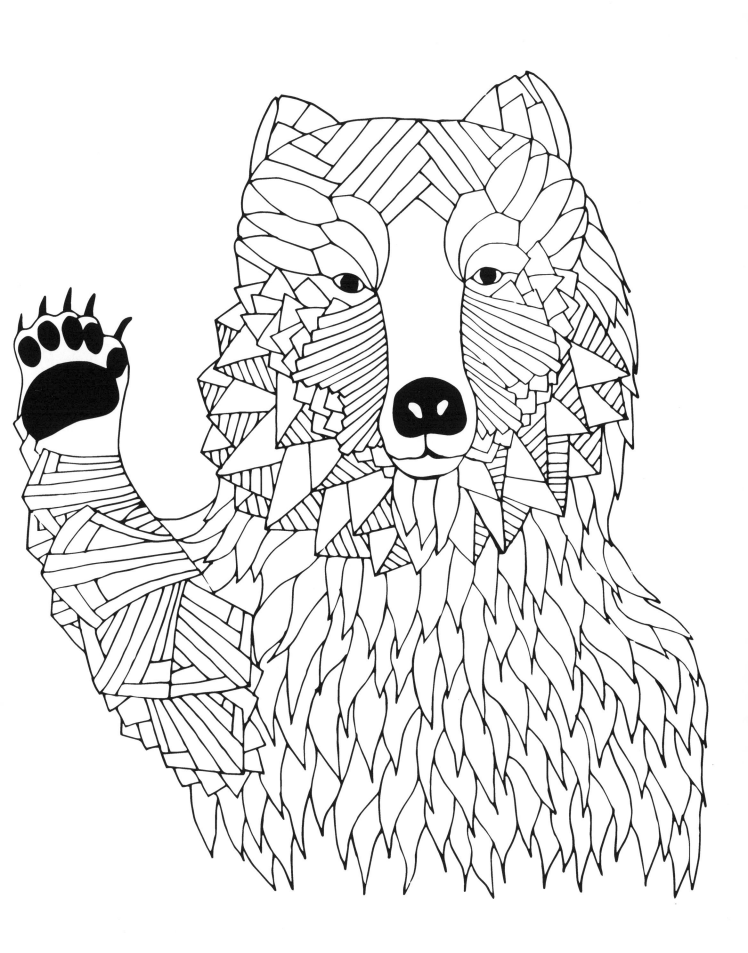

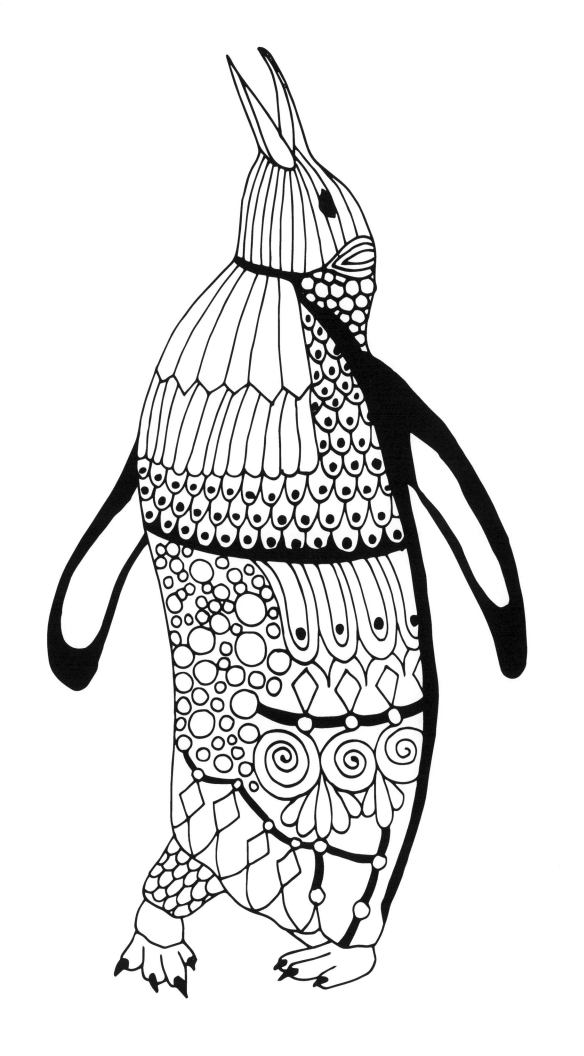

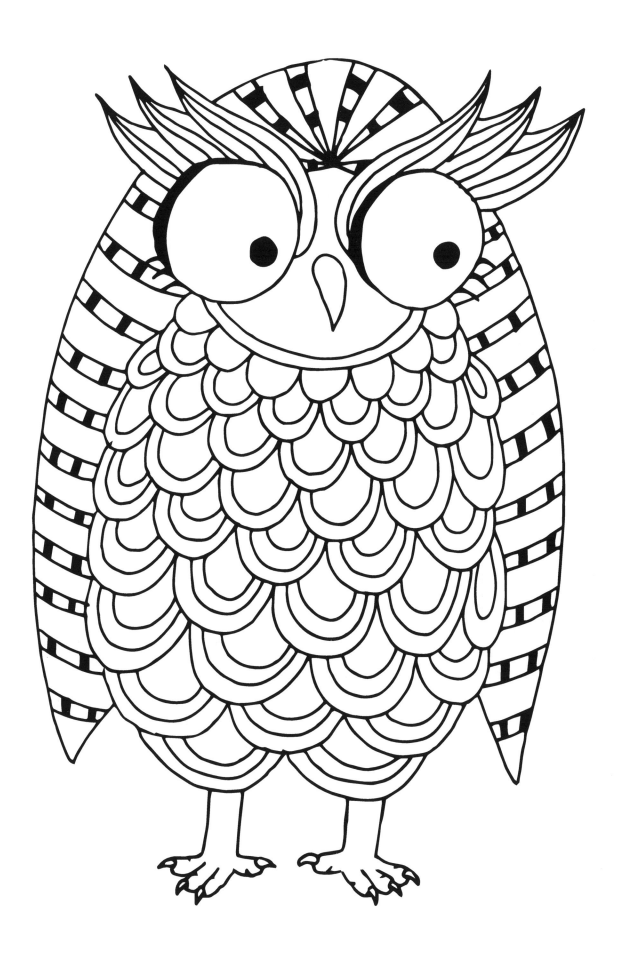

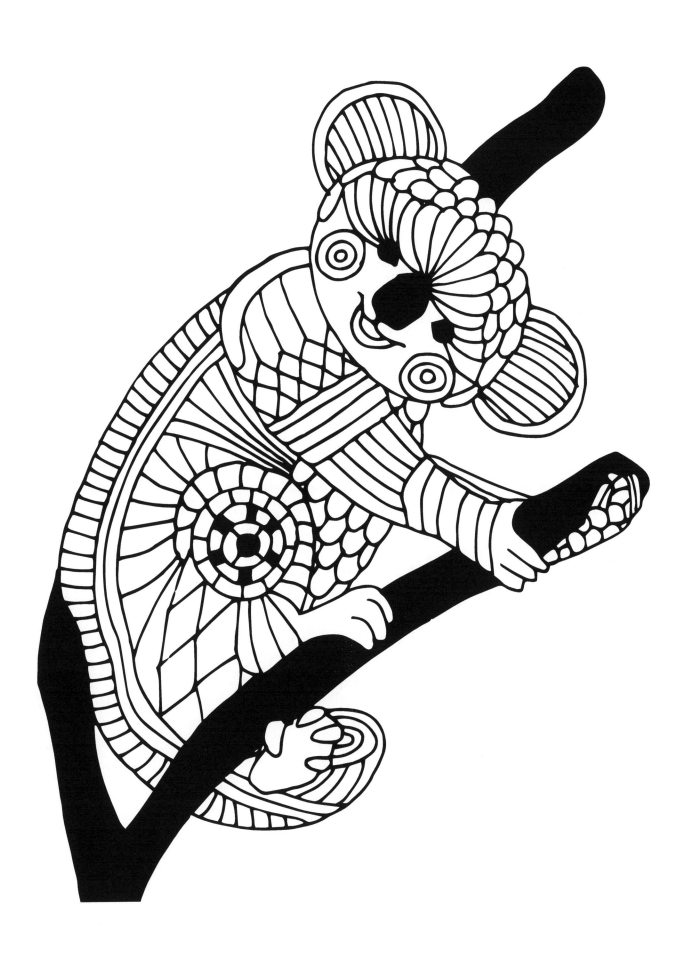

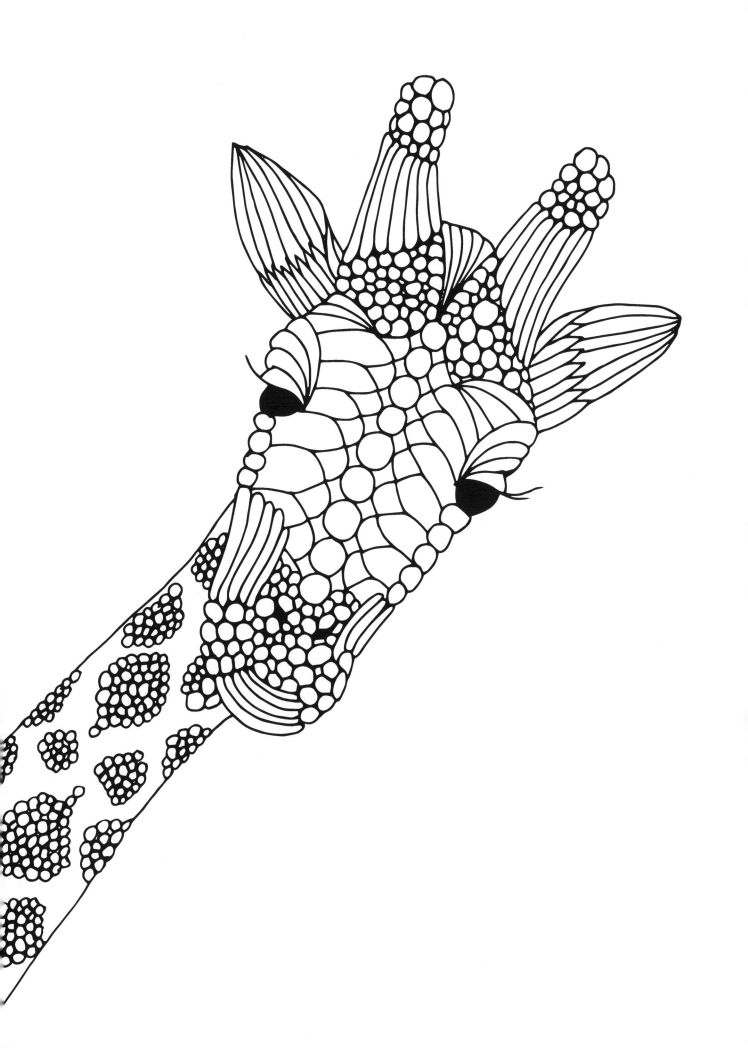

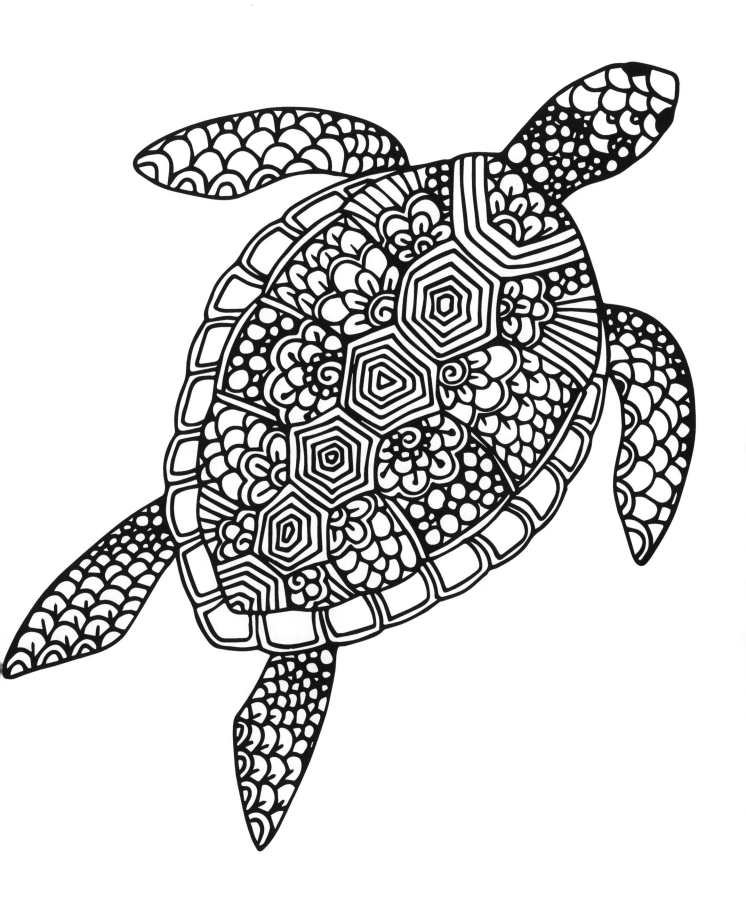

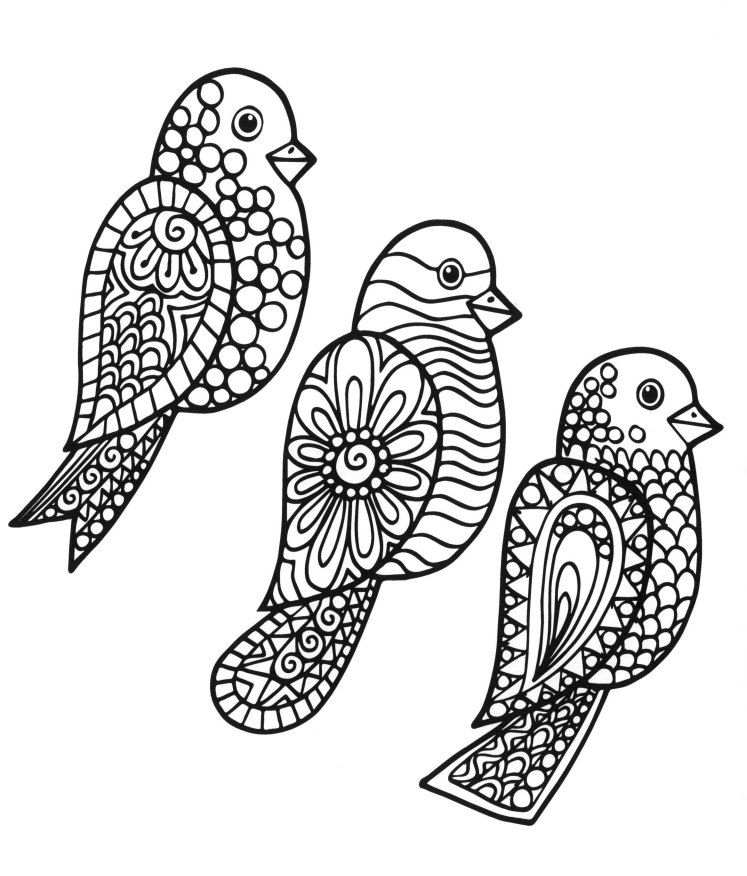

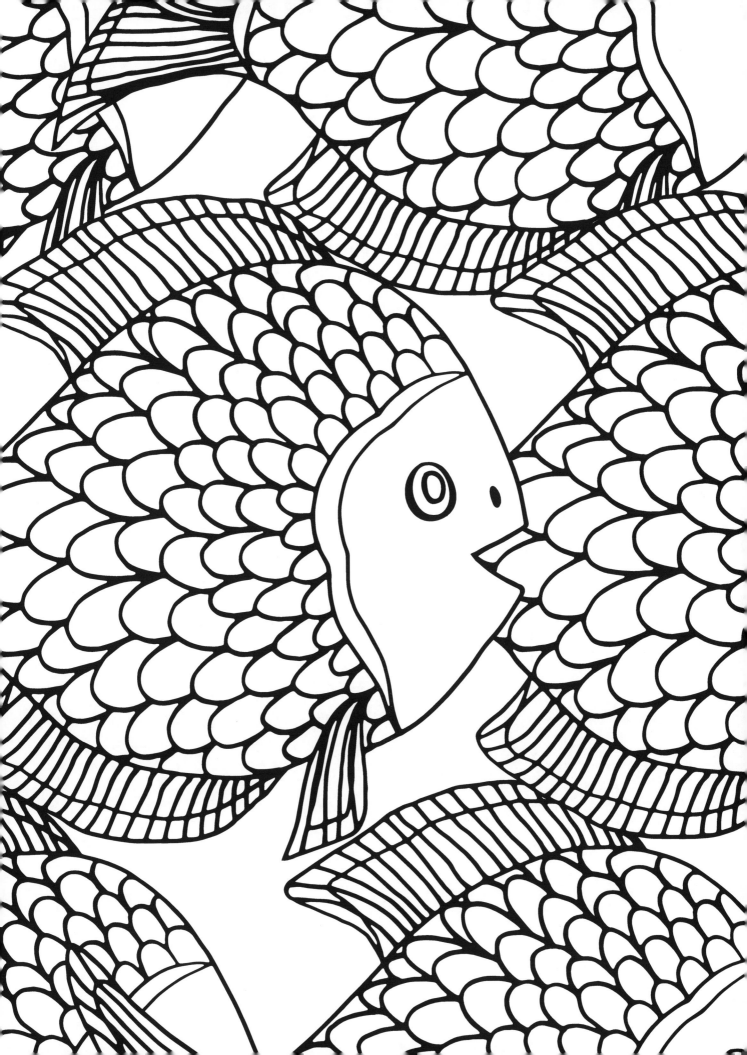

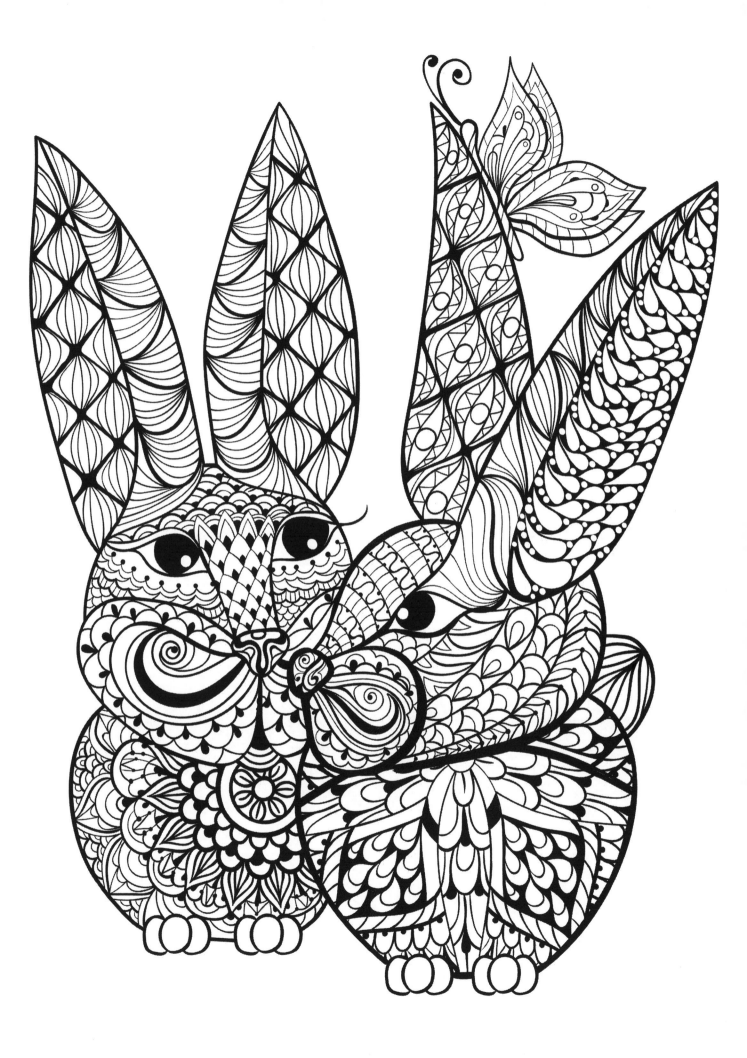

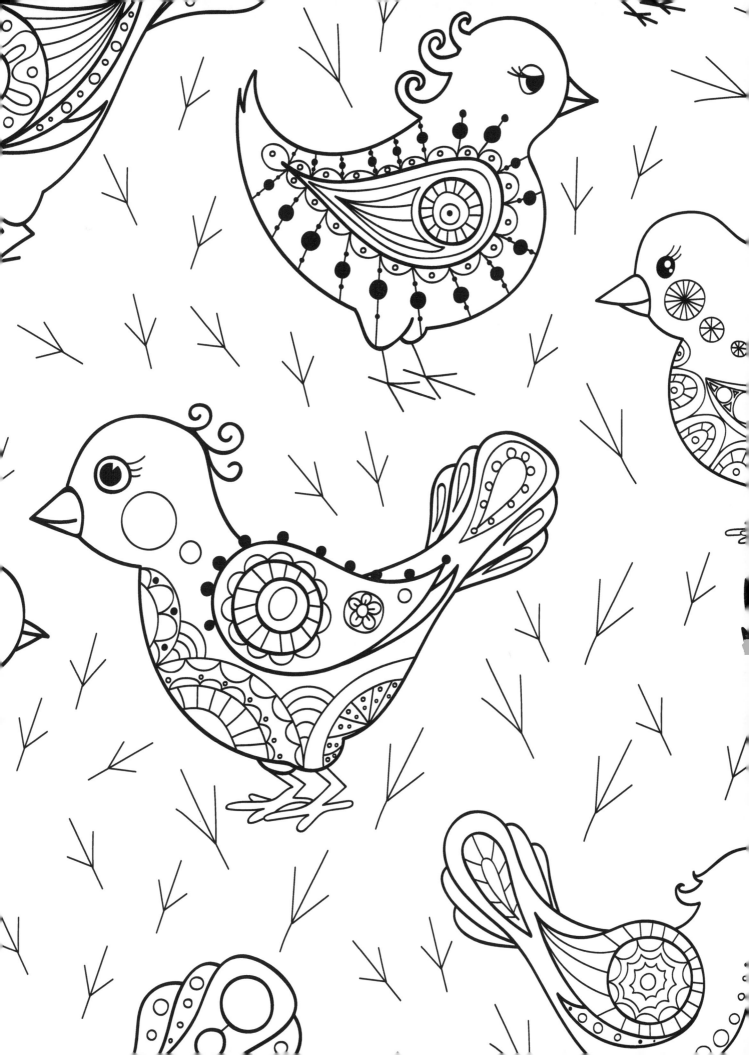

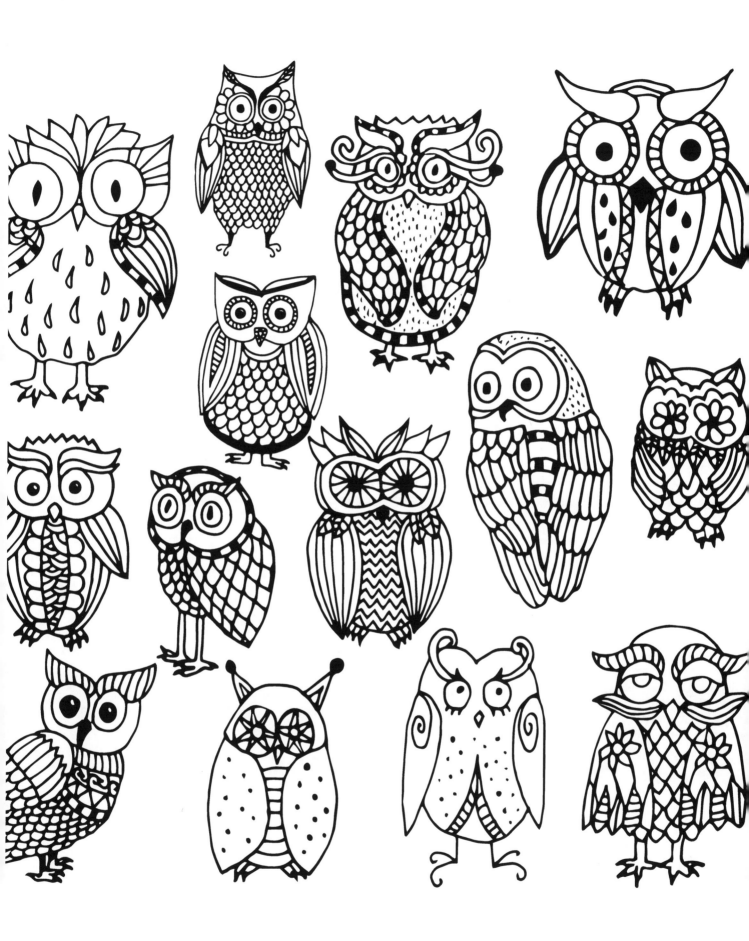

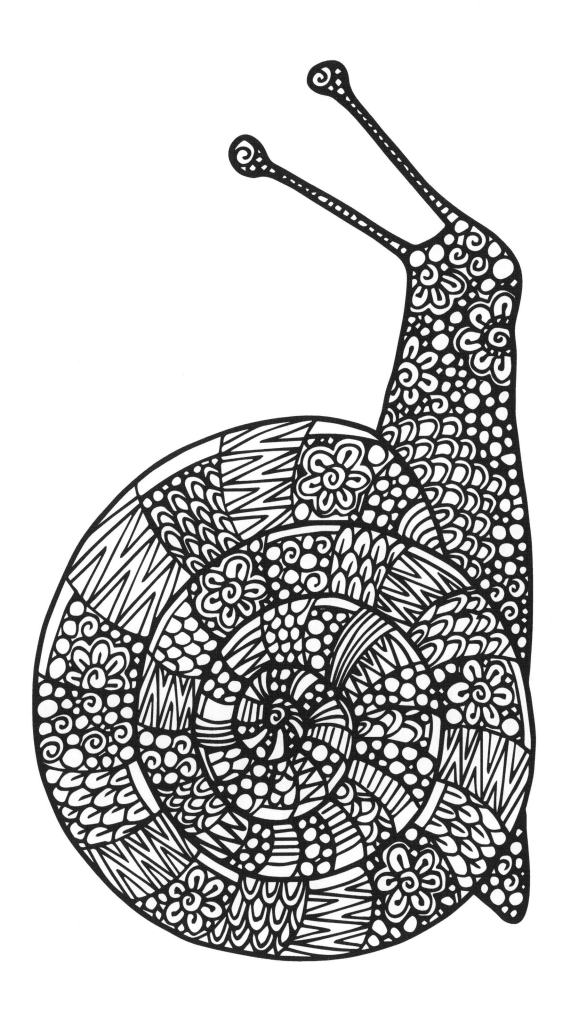

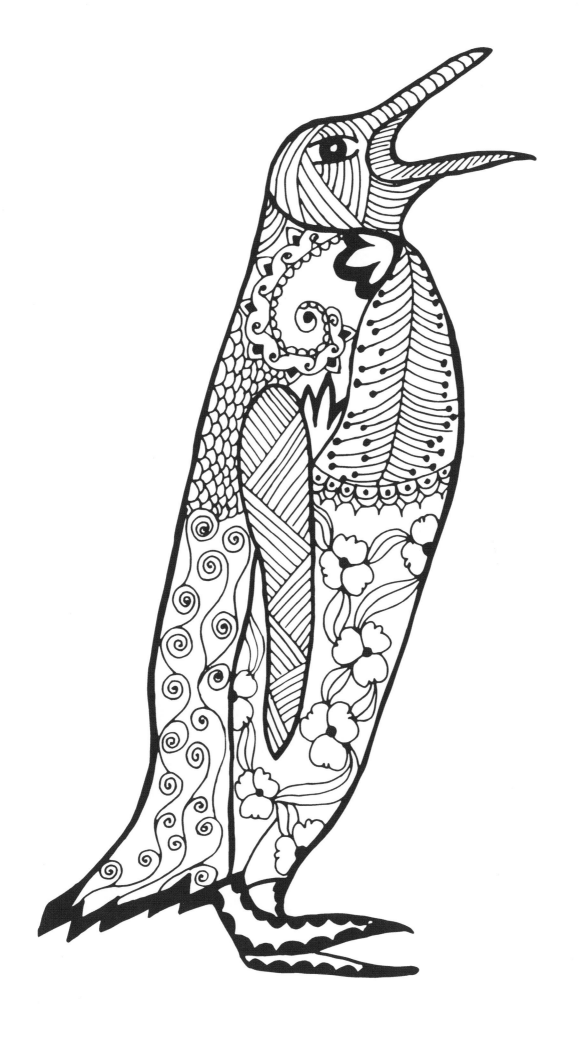

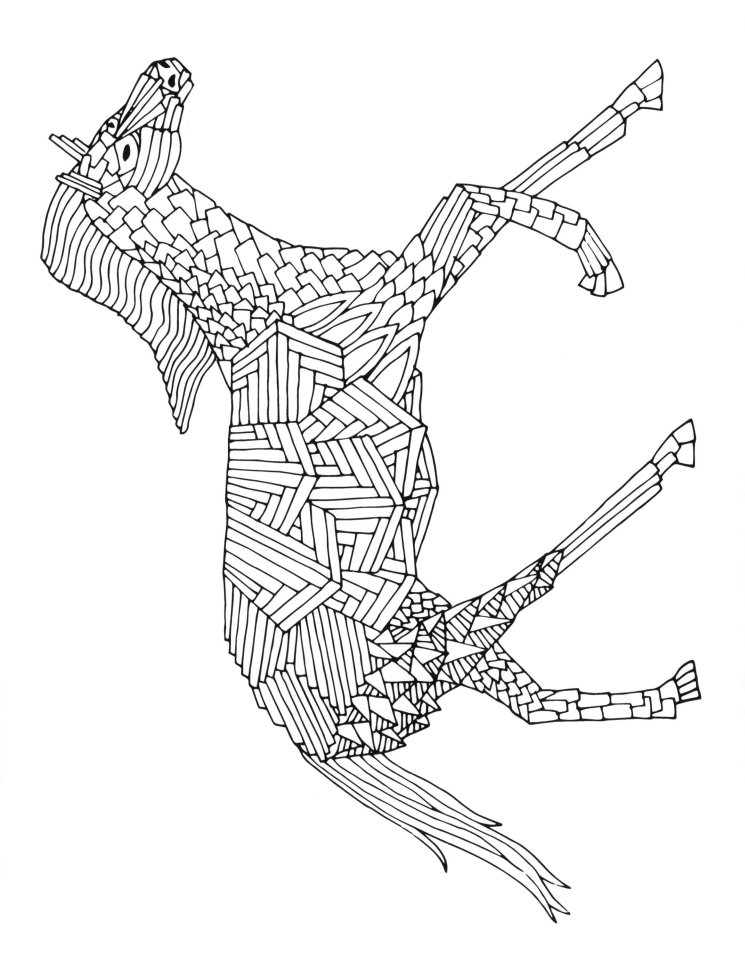

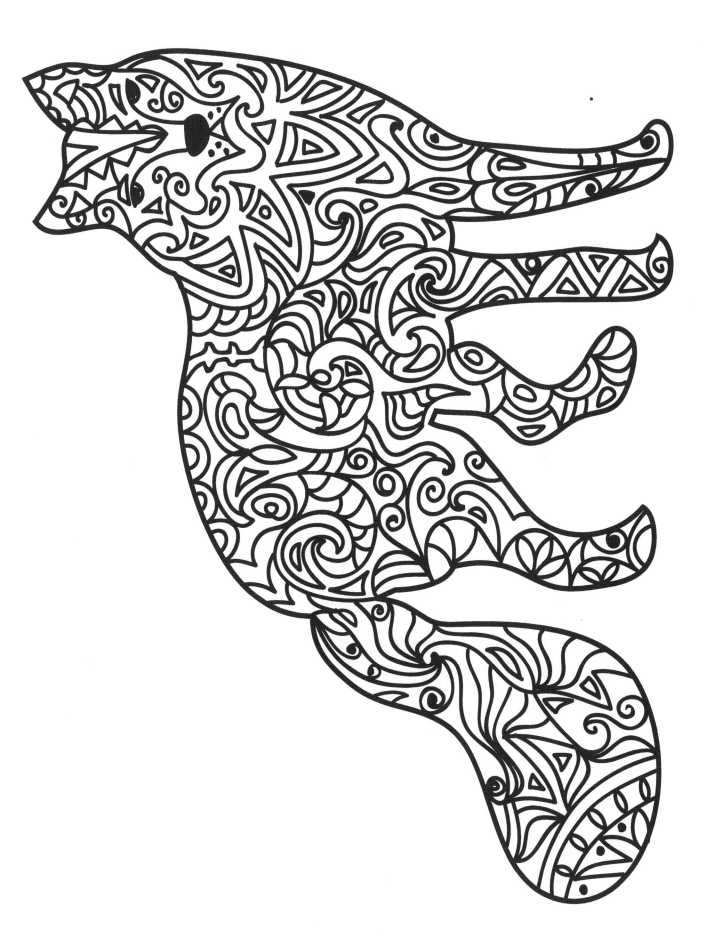

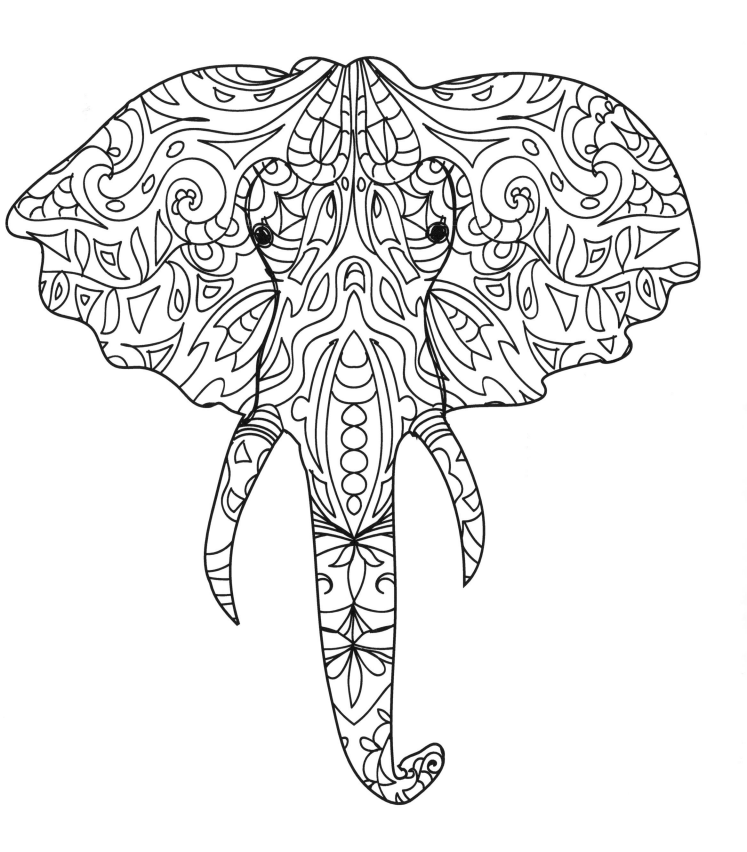

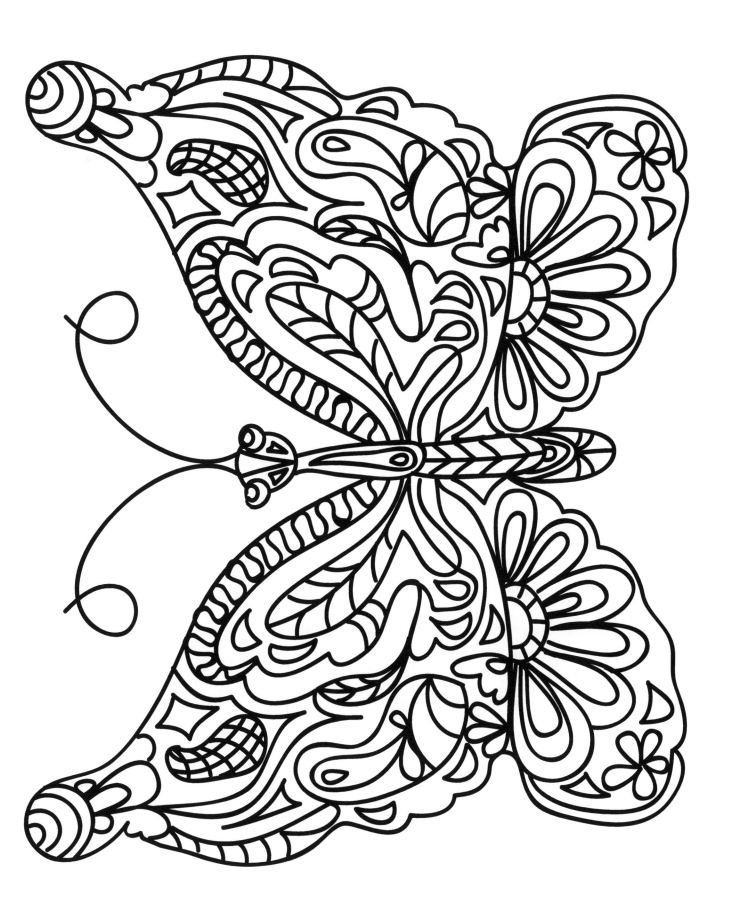

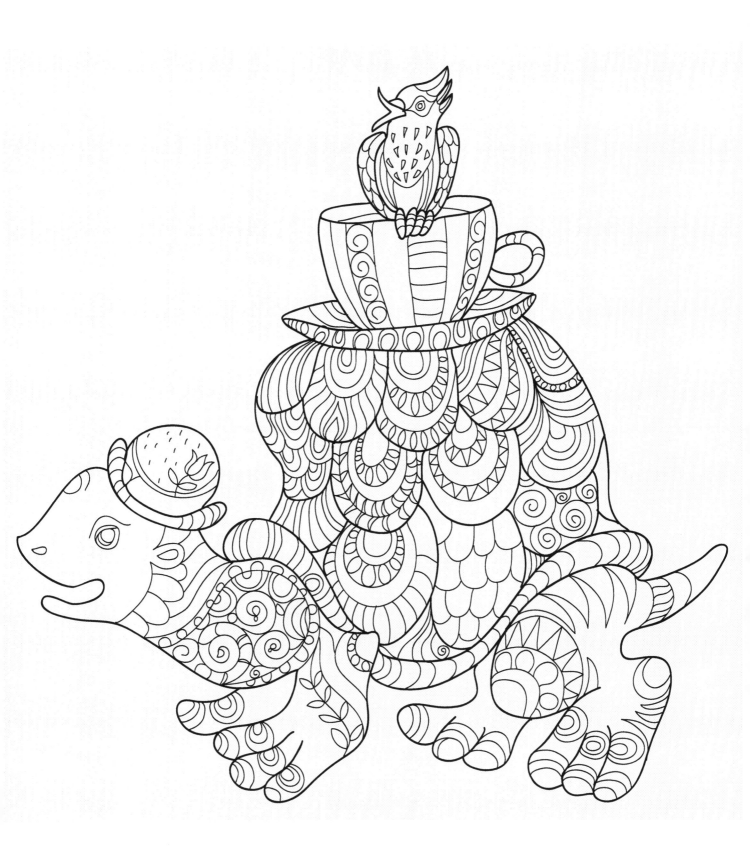

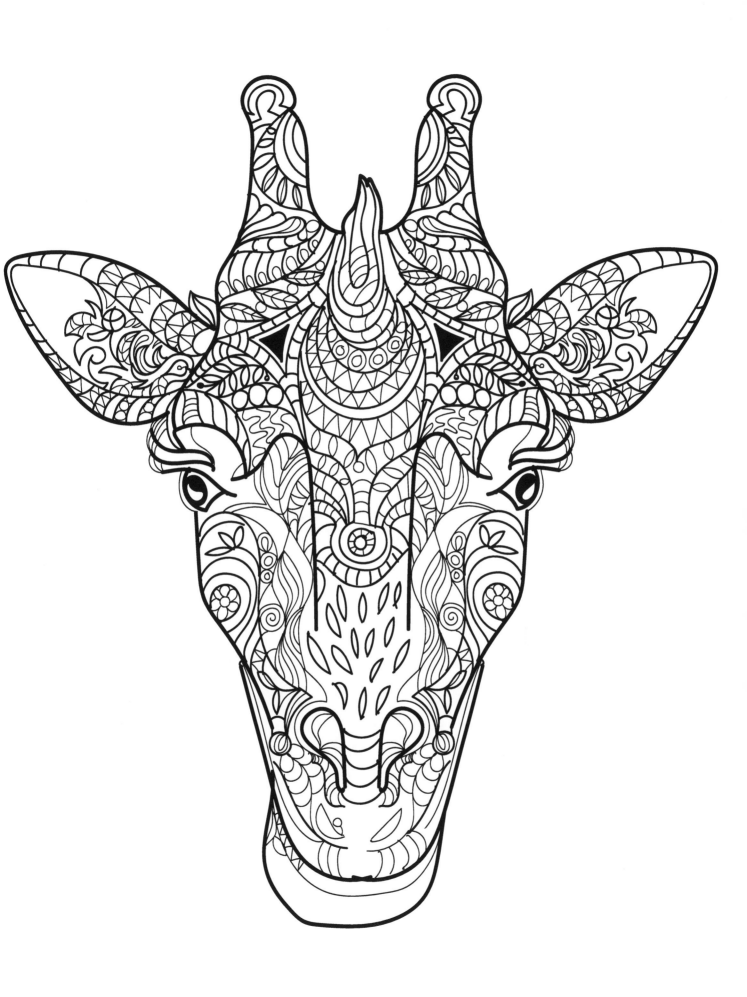

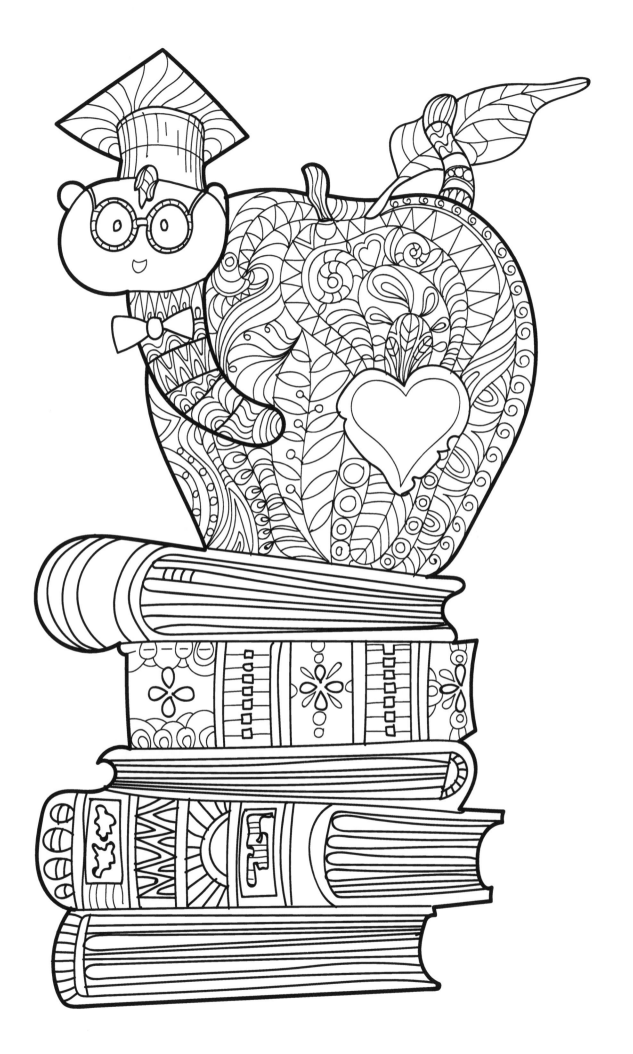

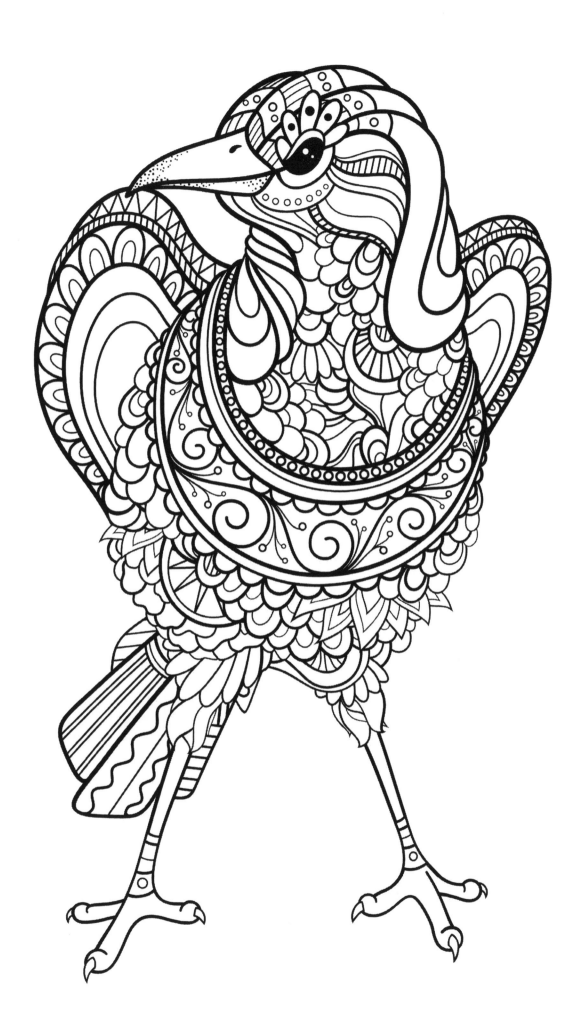

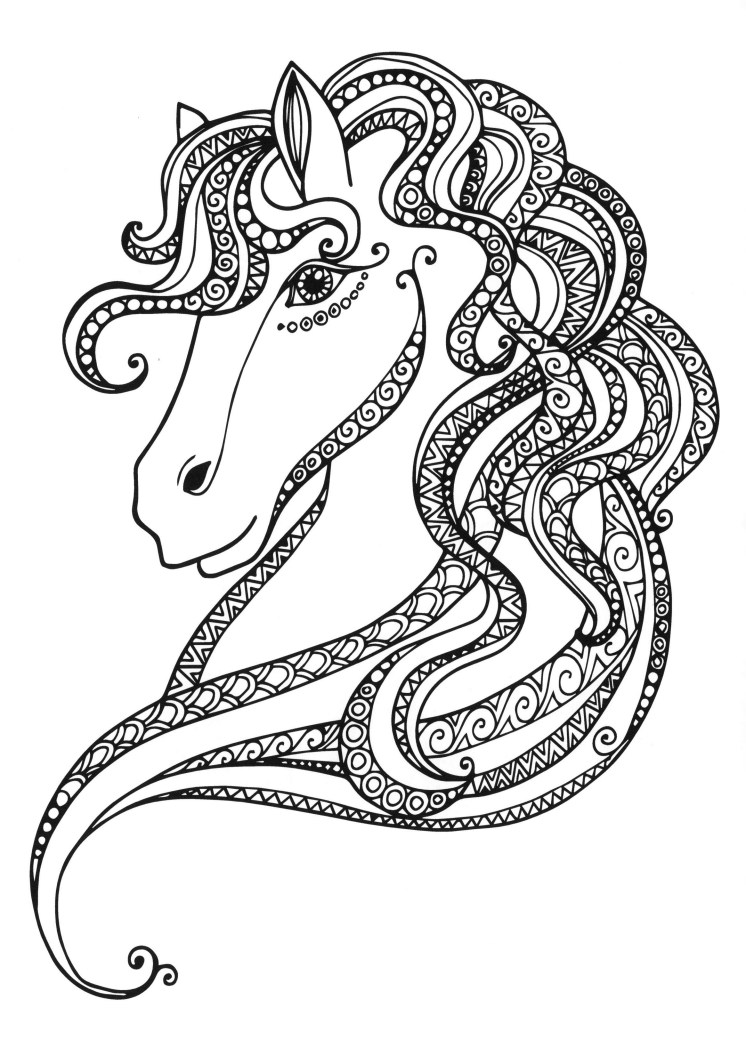

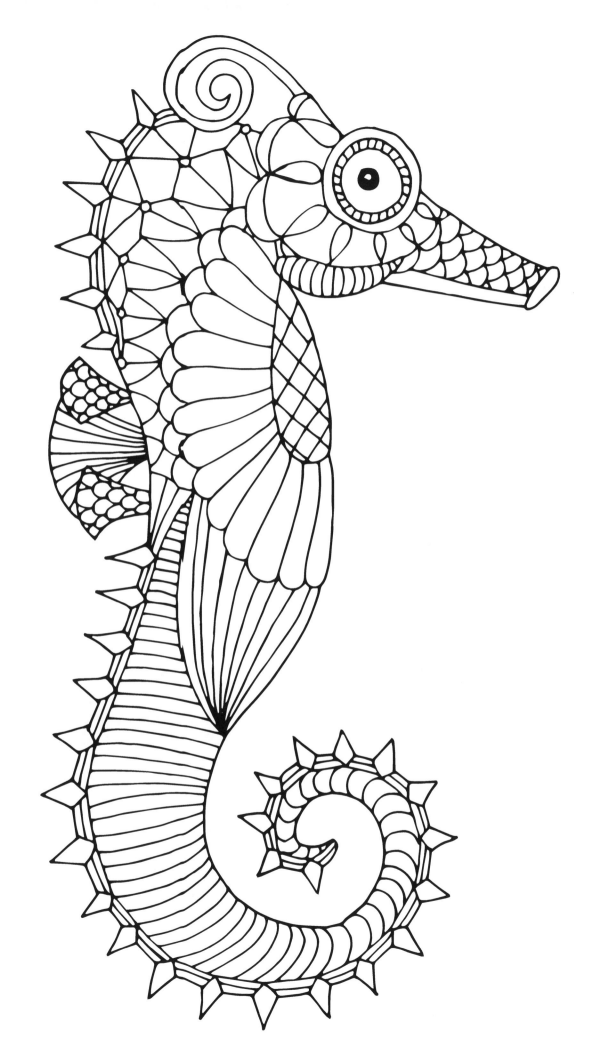

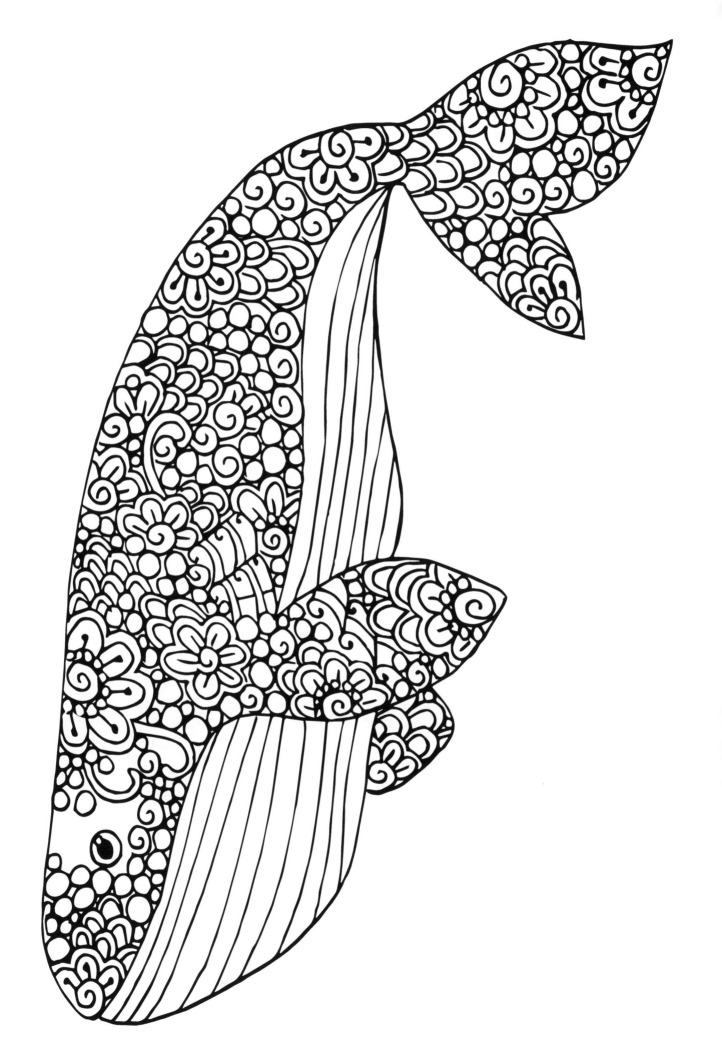

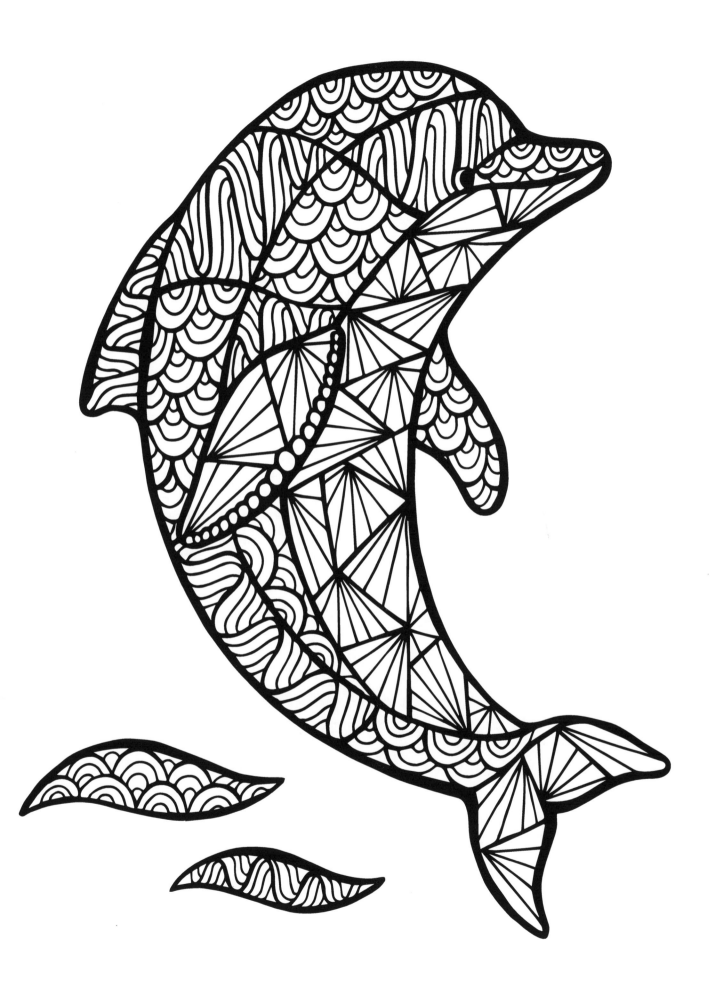

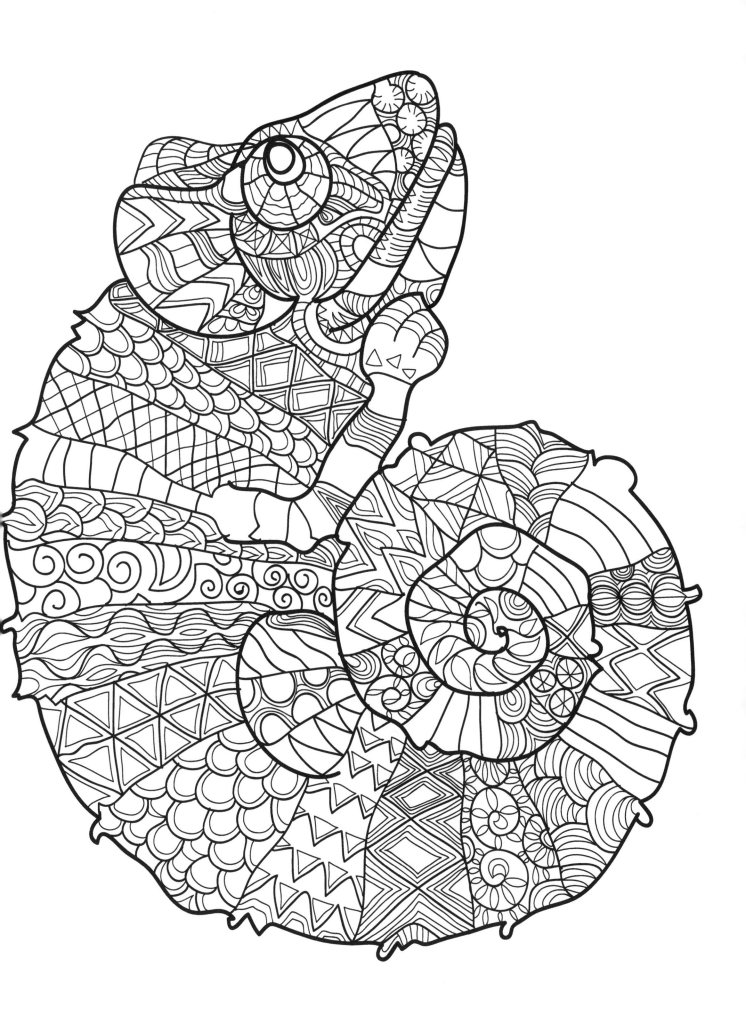

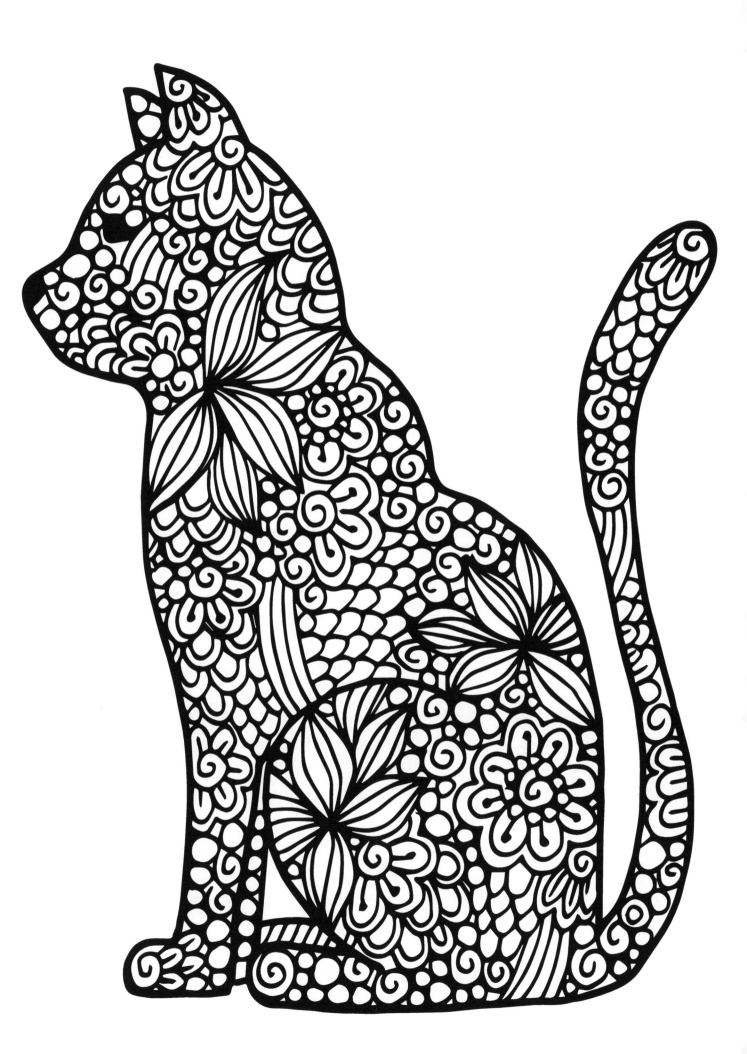

Printed in Great Britain
by Amazon.co.uk, Ltd.,
Marston Gate.